LIFT YOURSELF
21-DAY CHALLENGE

*The one-day-at-a-time guide to
having it all without losing yourself*

Copyright © 2016 by June Pinkney

This book is available at quantity discounts for bulk purchases.

All rights reserved. No part of this book may be reproduced or transmitted in any form or by any means, electronic or mechanical, including photocopying, recording, or any information storage and retrieval system, without written permission of the publisher except for brief quotations used in reviews, written specifically for inclusion in newspapers, blogs, or magazines.

ISBN-10:0-9741540-8-3

ISBN-13:978-0-9741540-8-4

Also available as an ebook on Amazon.com.

Printed in the United States of America

Dedication

For Pop-Pop (Daddy)
1933-2015

You are still my greatest inspiration. Thank you.

Contents

Introduction	9
LIFT Moments	14
LIFT Yourself 21-day Challenge	37
Acknowledgments	97

Introduction

Breast cancer took my mom's life when I was young, and the important life lessons she taught me at her bedside as she lay dying have woven their way into the woman I am today. She didn't want me to fall apart in a crisis; she wanted me to summon the courage to carry on while holding her close in my heart. When my dad passed recently, my whole world should have shattered once again. Of course, I was massively devastated to lose him. But like my mom, it was as if he was telling me to live strong. He left behind a treasure trove of personal notes that gave me a glimpse into his stoic toughness, a quality he undoubtedly had passed on to me. Even in death, my parents felt closer to me than I ever could have imagined. I realized that they had instilled in me a certain fortitude that has helped me through difficult times in my life. What seemed like a blow losing both parents, actually had the effect of strengthening me instead of breaking me. No longer the scared little girl worried about losing her mom, I had become a woman who was steely eyed in the face of life's storms, and I was certain, by God's grace, I could rise above the clouds.

I hadn't always dealt with adversity with strength. My mom certainly had planted the seeds, and my dad was beginning to water the tough mental core that would eventually anchor me. One day as I was going through my dad's things shortly after he passed, I noticed all of these handwritten note cards with encouraging quotes on them. He apparently jotted the notes to encourage himself during the challenging times in his life. They were in his wallet and his nightstand and he even had sticky notes and index cards posted all over his bedroom, on the walls and taped to his dresser mirror. Ironically, the messages my dad had written to encourage himself were now speaking words of comfort to me.

Some of the cards made me laugh because my dad was a horrible speller and I had to painstakingly decipher what he was trying to say. There was one card that stood out to me the most and the words made me examine my entire existence. Quoting Gandhi, the card read, "Live like you are going to die tomorrow and die like your are going to live forever." Perhaps he had been compelled to jot down that quote when my mom was near death, and he was forced to contemplate his own mortality some day. Did he have regrets about how he had lived his life? What things were still left undone on his bucket list?

As I pondered his many note cards, I had to admit to myself that I had not been living my life the way I had dreamed. Sure, I was doing what appeared to be the "right" thing: I graduated from college, I landed a great job as an accountant for a major insurance firm and I was moving up the corporate ranks and eventually earned my MBA. I was a self-sufficient adult. But was I living my dream? To answer that question, I embarked on a journey of self-reflection, and in the process I decided to LIFT myself from the state

Introduction

of just existing to the place of fulfilling my purpose.

I discovered that my passion was to help people deal with challenges in their lives. I had been a mentor to my nieces and nephews, guiding them through college and career goals, job searches and finances. Just as I had helped them to make important decisions and navigate life's crossroads, I wanted to reach out in the same way to women in business who sought greater fulfillment in their lives.

This book is designed to help professional women at a crossroads, those who feel accomplished yet unfulfilled in other areas and want to fill that gap in their lives. It is a call to action for women who are contemplating career moves or entrepreneurial endeavors but don't know where to start. Those are the women who will benefit most from this self-help guide, written by a woman who has successfully faced the same challenges and demands.

Many professional women are comfortable taking on leadership roles or building a company, but they don't apply those same principles of success to their personal lives. Many of us seek greater personal satisfaction outside of our careers, but we don't always take the time to laser-focus on the bigger vision for our lives. Sometimes we get so bogged down with the challenges of daily life, that we bury our inner hopes and dreams. I created a process for working through challenges while staying focused on your personal goals.

LIFT, an acronym for Living in Freedom and Truth, helps women to identify their higher calling in life, so to speak.

The LIFT Yourself 21-day Challenge is designed to show you that you can always LIFT yourself to a higher level of personal fulfillment.

By reflecting on your past, examining your present situation and mapping out your future, you will gain a clear-eyed picture of the old you vs. the new you. How long have you wanted to replace the faded you with the new and improved version? How many times have you told yourself that it's too late or too big a task to head in a completely new direction in life? Well, it never hurts to try. It never hurts to have a plan in place for when you finally make that leap to the next level of your life.

Spend the next 21 days on an introspective journey learning to put your personal goals first. In addition to the space provided after each question, you can use a notebook or journal to write down additional thoughts and revelations. Each day there is a principle to reflect on, an explanation or demonstration of the principle and related questions for you to answer. I share my own journal reflections to inspire you to share your own story, so that you can LIFT a woman in your circle of influence.

The questions are designed to get you to reflect on the lessons that you've learned. Take the time to document your thoughts during this challenge. Keeping a log of your thoughts and experiences has many benefits, but one of the best is being able to look back and see your thoughts and ideas months or years from now. You will be able to see your growth and progress and identify areas where you need

INTRODUCTION

to make adjustments. I share with you some of my journal entries from the year 2000 throughout this book.

When I looked back at my journal, I saw areas where I had major growth and other areas where I was still stuck in the same place 16 years later. I am grateful that I had captured those memories, because they allowed me to be able to share in detail with you the principles I learned through my own LIFT process.

LIFT will take you through a process of self-reflection and goal-setting to get you to the place you are destined to be. For some, arriving at your destiny may require making some major life changes, and for others it will mean learning to put yourself first or learning to enjoy the wonderful life you have created. Wherever you are in your journey, I am confident that you will find some tips and tools to LIFT your life to a new level.

FIVE STRATEGIES FOR MAXIMUM RESULTS FROM THIS BOOK

1. Read it. Reflect on it. Take action.
2. Write down your top five quotes on an index card or in your phone and study them.
3. Share your favorite quotes and insights on the LIFT social media sites. This resource will help other women find the strength they need to LIFT.
4. Share your favorite quotes and insights on your personal social media sites. This will spark

conversations that may help other women you are connected to.

5. Re-read the book whenever you need a quick LIFT.

The pages of my life have been eventful, but through it all I never felt like life dealt me a bad hand. This revelation is the true essence of LIFT. I want to use my life experiences to help other women live their best lives by learning from my mistakes, experiences and revelations. In an effort to do so I am going to share with you the crucial events in my life that pushed me to want to teach women to LIFT themselves.

LIFT Moments

I look at my life as a series of events that have all helped to mold me into the woman that I am today. Each situation taught me that I am in control of how I allow circumstances to shape me and my life. In sharing this lesson, I want to empower women from all walks of life.

Life is a gift from God but life doesn't always go the way we planned it. Sometimes we go through life asking the question, "Why?"

Why did my mom have to get sick and die before she got to see me grow up? Why didn't my mom live long enough to see my son? Why did my life never go the way everyone else's went? Why did I have to go to Catholic school when everyone else went to public

INTRODUCTION

school? Why was I always so different?

Why is life so complicated and why are there so many questions and not enough answers?

Perhaps it was because God desired for me to trust Him, reach out to Him and rest in Him? Each day that I live I realize that the things that I experienced weren't a punishment but they were part of God's plan for my life. God wanted to use me and He knew that before I was conceived that I would help people. He set my life up so that circumstances would make me seek Him.

I didn't have a mother to lean on. There is a big age difference between my siblings and me. I am the youngest of five children, and there is an eight-year age difference between me and my brother and a 20-year age difference between me and my oldest sister. My mother had my oldest sister at 16 and me at 36. I never really trusted people enough to share my deepest feelings with them. God knew he had to teach me to be able to stand alone.

I was always different. As the youngest child I was extremely spoiled. My dad gave me whatever I wanted, whenever I wanted it. If I didn't feel like walking, he would carry me. I remember I was very picky about my food. My sandwiches had to be cut in four triangles, and I refused to eat the sandwich if it was not sliced exactly right. My mom did not suffer my pickiness and expected me to eat the sandwich however she made it, but my dad would always save the day and make me a new sandwich just the way I liked it.

There are so many other examples of my dad going out of his way to make sure that I was happy. My dad was not working when I was born; he was on permanent medical disability so he was home with me all day. I spent my days sitting with him watching TV, doing laundry, cooking dinner and cleaning the house. I was always right by his side. I was daddy's little girl. My older sisters and brother were enjoying their lives, so my dad became my playmate because there was no one else around. My mom did not have time for that kind of child's play; she had been there, done that with my older siblings. I was an unexpected pregnancy, and by the time I was born, she was too worn out to make time to play. My brother and sister also spoiled me because I was the baby. To my mom, I was her showpiece; she would dress me up everyday and take pictures of me. I have a million pictures of me growing up yet my siblings struggle to find pictures from their childhood. For as long as I can remember my mom would tell me that I was special and that I was going to do great things in life. So I grew up believing this. My mother's words of encouragement shaped my entire view of myself.

I was the only African-American child in my elementary school from 1st-7th grade, being the sole black child was not a obstacle. It exposed me to a whole different world socially and economically. I visited my friends' mansions and vacation homes and my eyes were opened to another realm of possibilities. Experiencing the lifestyle of wealthy people made me dream big about the life I wanted when I became an adult.

Introduction

My home life was the complete opposite. I lived in public housing with no car and just the bare necessities. Yet I was blessed to be able to experience the best of two different worlds, and my dual point of view helped me to develop into an open-minded adult. I was able to achieve academic success in school while maintaining my cultural identity. My friends assumed I would start to talk and act differently because I attended Catholic school but that did not happen. My mom worked at the church rectory to pay for a portion of my tuition, and my dad was on disability from his job so he also had some income. They were very frugal, which helped them to be able to afford my private school education.

During the 6th grade my mom was diagnosed with breast cancer. She had surgery and treatments and she seemed OK for about a year. Then they told us that the cancer had returned and she had to have a double mastectomy. This time my mom never fully recovered. She had to undergo chemotherapy, lost her hair and started to lose a lot of weight. When my mom got sick, all I could do was pray to God. I should not have known God as intimately as I did. Even though my mom was Catholic and my dad was Baptist, they did not go to church. Looking back, I know that God had his hand on me even as a young child.

As mom progressively got worse, I watched how my dad took care of her, noting that he had to do more and more for her. I watched how he loved my mom as she was dying and at the same time he protected us from the harsh reality that she was getting worse. I remember talking to God at night and praying that he would make my mom better. As time went on, even though I was young, I knew that my mom would never get better. I watched her get thinner and thinner and weaker until I could no longer be selfish and pray for what I wanted. But I began to pray to God that he would give my mom peace, and I knew peace meant she might have to go to heaven. I wanted her to be free from the pain.

I would sit with my mom all day long and she would tell me stories and give me advice about life. She was on serious medication and sometimes she would say things that made no sense, but that did not change my love for her. Later, I tried to forget those bad times and instead remember all the advice she had given me in the short time we had together. I love her so much and I thank her for everything she gave me. She taught me to love and to be tough. She told me I was special and I could be anything I wanted in life. She gave me a desire to go on even without her.

When my mom passed my mom's family was very mean and bitter towards my dad. They spoke badly about him and they didn't even show up to her memorial service. In spite of the way they treated my dad he never spoke one harsh word about them. Me on the other hand, I let it be known that if they did not like my dad, they did not like me. Unfortunately, I never regained a relationship with my grandmother or my aunt. Despite the pain my dad felt as he buried the woman he loved, he never missed a beat. He kept going because he knew we needed him. My dad remained strong during the toughest period of his life because his children needed him. I learned so much from my dad during that experience. I believe that is why I was able to handle the things that came my way in life with such strength and poise. I learned that you do not have to treat people the way they treat you. I learned that God will take you through the toughest times in your life. Most of all I learned that true love is not selfish.

Prior to my mom's illness, I never thought I would be able to make it in life without her. I would hear people say that they could not make it without their mom, so I started to adopt that mindset until I was faced with the reality of watching her struggle with her illness and realized it was selfish of me to feel that way. However when she passed God sent His angels to watch over me and to help me accept that I must go on without my mom. I remember praying every night for the strength to make it through the next day. I remember I was counting the days that I made it after her death, and before I knew it a month had passed, then six months, then a year. With each passing day that I was able to survive, I knew that God was truly real because he was the reason I was able to survive. Even when I didn't know God, he gave me the strength and comfort I needed to go on, day by day.

Now I know that God deals with us even before we fully recognize him, because how else could I have learned to pray with such sincerity and without pretense. I prayed to God like I was talking to my best friend. My family was not a family that prayed together. God placed the gift of prayer in me when I was young because he knew that prayer would be the very thing that saved my life.

I was in the 8th grade when my mom passed away so she didn't get to see me graduate from 8th grade and go to high school; these milestones were among the most important things to her. I was determined to go to high school, graduate and go to college for my mom. I knew I had to stay focused on my education and not boys because she had drilled that in my head. She told me to get my education first, I had plenty of time for boys later. All of my sisters lost their focus in school, and got caught up with boys. I was able to make it through high school, graduating at the top of my class. I was accepted to several colleges but I chose to attend Drexel and live on campus because I didn't want to be too far from my dad. I felt like I had made my mom proud.

Embracing Single Motherhood

I worked in the accounting department at a bookstore for my internship in college. I will never forget the day he entered my life. I was sitting at my desk at work and he walked in the office, laughing and joking with the other employees. I sat there trying not to stare but very much interested in finding out who he was. There was one problem; I was shy so I did not even know how to go about approaching him. So day after day I would sit at my desk and anxiously wait for him to come into my office to drop off paperwork to one of the other employees. Silently, I was hoping he would notice me but I wasn't confident that would happen. As the weeks went on I finally found the courage to ask my co-worker

INTRODUCTION

who he was. I don't know why I did that because I knew I was never going to approach him and he was too popular to notice me. Then it happened, I was sitting at my desk and the work phone rang, I knew something was wrong because my phone never rang. I answered it and as soon as I heard the voice on the other end, my heart raced. It was him and he wanted to know if he could have my home phone number. From that moment on, my life was never the same. We began to spend all of our free time together and I was mesmerized and madly in love with him. I am pretty confident that he felt the same about me; actually his feelings may have been even stronger. This relationship became the focus of my life. I stopped going to college parties with my friends. He and I were always together.

Imagine sitting at the desk at your semester-long internship in your second semester of sophomore year in college and you cannot keep your eyes open. In between dozing off, your mind is racing because you have never felt so tired before and you remember that your cycle is late. You can't really focus on anything because you know you have prolonged getting a pregnancy test for as long as you can. To make matters worse, you know you need to go to the doctor because you are almost certain you are pregnant and you need more than a pregnancy test. You are scared to go to your family doctor and use your dad's health insurance because you don't want anyone to know if you are pregnant. This is what happened to me. I knew I could not delay it any longer so I went to the doctor. Just as I suspected, the test came back positive, and in that moment my entire life took a major shift.

When I was certain I was pregnant with my son, I was so excited but I was also deeply concerned. My deepest concern was that I hadn't finished college. I didn't have a job so I was not financially stable. I knew that he would be a blessing to me and that I would be an amazing mom. I was determined that my son would not suffer for my poor planning. I received a lot of negative feedback regarding my pregnancy from my family and friends, but it pushed me to finish my degree. This determination drove me to continue taking classes all the way up until my delivery date. Now that might not seem like a big deal but it was for me. Traveling on public transportation for more than an hour was challenging. It was November in Philadelphia and I hate the cold. I remember the last month of my pregnancy was the worst. I was exhausted due to the additional weight and even though it was winter, I was overheating in my coat due to pregnancy hot flashes.

My close girlfriends told me to just drop my classes. "It is too much for you," they would tell me, seeing my fatigue from traveling back and forth to class and late nights studying. But I was determined; I thought about the lifestyle I wanted and decided that I was going to class as long as I could make it there physically. I had the whole thing planned out. My due date was two weeks after the fall semester would end so I would be able to finish the semester, have the baby and go back to class in January. I was unwavering. Nothing was going to stop me. My plan did not work out so well because my son came early, but he was gracious enough to come over Thanksgiving break. I was able to complete the work for the

INTRODUCTION

last week of class at home and take exams. I successfully completed all my exams except the last one because I had the time wrong and I missed it. I was consumed with my new baby. I am happy to say that I still passed the class with an "A," and I am confident it was because the professor saw my dedication and determination to finish even while I was nine months pregnant. Whenever life would present challenges that made me want to quit or make excuses, I would think back to that time and remind myself if I could make it through that semester, then there was nothing that I could not accomplish.

My desire for results overpowered my desire to give up. So whenever you are tempted to make an excuse, remember a time when your determination helped you reach an impossible goal. If you can't recall a story of your own then remember the fat, hot, pregnant lady that went to class all the way up to her delivery date.

My son's dad and I had the best time of our lives during my pregnancy despite the fact that most people were disappointed in us. In their opinion we were too young to have a child. It was us against the world and that was just fine. We had plans to get married once we got established and settled. When our son was born, that was the greatest moment of both of our lives. Our little family was just perfect, we didn't have a big house and fancy cars but we had each other.

Then life happened and reality set in; we had a child to provide for so things were not always fun. I was a planner and he was creative free spirit, so our worlds collided, not physically, but emotionally. The one thing we always agreed on was our desire to provide our son with all the things we did not have growing up.

Our relationship gradually shifted to just a friendship. Our family and friends did not even realize there was a transition. After a few months without seeing us together all of the time, they started asking questions. That was a painful time in my life, a major heartache. I had broken up with the love of my life. I felt like a complete failure because I'd had a baby and he would have to be raised in a single-parent home. I didn't know how to recover from the end of the relationship. I remember talking to my girlfriends about the situation, but those conversations just made me more depressed.

I resolved that I had to find a way to get myself together because my son was dependent on me. I went on a self-improvement journey. It was during that process that I resolved to do whatever it took to develop a great career and build the best life possible for myself and my son. I had to put the pain aside and look for the lesson in the story.

My son's dad and I remained very good friends and resolved that we would raise our son together in peace and love. We promised each other that we would break every stereotype that existed about single parents. We did a great job at achieving this goal, as my son was able to have both of his parents actively involved in his life and we were not fussing and fighting. Now do not get me wrong, we did have disagreements but we never allowed the world to see those times.

This relationship with my son's dad had the biggest impact on my life. I learned how to love unconditionally. At first he was the love of my life and then my biggest heartbreak. Most importantly he was the father of my son, the true love of my life. I had no choice but to love him, because every time I looked at my son I saw him. Sometimes in your life you will have to look at your pain and the only way to deal with it will be to embrace it.

My Dad, My Best Friend

When I became a mom I also became a very light sleeper. The slightest noise would awaken me. At the time my dad, my son and I were living in the house together. My dad had a very rigid routine. He got up at the same time every day, and went to the bathroom to get dressed. Then I would hear him go downstairs to make his coffee. On this particular morning, I heard my dad go into the bathroom much earlier than normal. For some reason this bothered me so I couldn't really go back to sleep, I just lay in the bed. I soon realized that my dad had not gotten up at his normal time. I was very uneasy so I went to his room and knocked on the door and he didn't answer. I opened the door and he was lying on the bed struggling to breath. There was no time to panic; I called 911 and tried to get my dad to stay with me until help arrived. Simultaneously, I had to figure out what to do with my one-year-old baby who was in the other room. I called my neighbor and she ran over to help me and at the same time the ambulance arrived. They were able to get my dad breathing and transported him to the hospital.

After many tests and a few hours later, we learned that my dad had a blood clot in his right leg that had traveled to his lungs. If I had not found him when I did he would have died. I remember telling God that I was not ready to lose my dad; I needed him. Later that day, we also received some more devastating news, my dad only had one functioning kidney. His right kidney was blocked with a cancerous tumor and he had bladder cancer. I remember being devastated but I could not show it because my dad had such a positive outlook. He agreed to undergo surgery to remove his kidney and to begin treatment for the bladder cancer. The surgery for the kidney removal was a major surgery and to make matters worse my dad was 64 years old. We made it through the surgery and the chemotherapy for the bladder cancer as smoothly as could be expected. The chemotherapy for the bladder cancer was a direct treatment and did not make my dad too sick or make his hair fall out.

My dad was able to successfully beat the bladder cancer but due to the high recurrence rate, he had to go through a short procedure every four months to make sure it did not return. On one of our routine visits, I was sitting with my dad in the recovery room and I asked him if he believed in miracles and he said, "I don't know." I responded, "I do and I think God is going to show us a miracle." A minute

INTRODUCTION

later I looked at my dad and he was once again gasping for air. I yelled for the nurse and they came running in and began to work on him, his heart rate was rapidly decreasing. I remember praying to God once again, "Please don't take my dad. I need him." The doctors and nurses were able to get his blood pressure back up and he was right back to normal. They kept him in the hospital and ran more tests to determine the cause of the incident. They discovered that although my dad had been treated for epilepsy for most of his life, he did not, in fact, have epilepsy. The real problem was his heart but that condition was treatable. My dad went through the next few years without any more major medical events.

Going through these crises with my dad forced me to grow up and handle the responsibilities of the household. I was handling multiple responsibilities at the same time and I was only 22. Prior to my dad's illness he had been my childcare provider. So in the midst of taking care of my dad as he recovered from his surgery and chemotherapy, I had to find childcare for my son. I have other siblings who assisted when it was convenient, but the majority of my father's care was up to me because he lived with me. Looking back on those two years and the countless hours my son and I spent in hospital waiting rooms, working a full-time job and chasing a toddler, I am not sure how I survived. Dealing with all of these pressures of life did lead me to reconnect with God. I started praying and reading my Bible more because I needed His help to deal with all that I was dealing with. To this day, my family does not understand the magnitude of my responsibilities from age 22 to 25. It was truly the grace of God that equipped me to handle the pressure of that period of my life.

In November 2007, my dad went in for his routine physical and we received news that the cancer had returned. The doctors wanted to perform a surgery to remove my dad's bladder. The surgery would have been 18 hours long and there was little chance that my dad could handle that surgery at 74 years old. So my dad opted for radiation and the intravenous chemotherapy. I watched my dad embrace this treatment with strength and determination. The only downside was that his bladder was no longer functioning so he had to get a nephrostomy tube that emptied into a leg bag. I knew this was devastating for my dad but he embraced the process like it was no big deal. The radiation treatments went fine and he started the chemotherapy, but this time things were different. I had moved out and my sister and her children were staying with my dad. I was getting calls that my dad would not get out of the bed and he was not eating. I would have to go over and make him eat. I was the youngest, but I knew just what to do to get my dad to eat.

I remember watching him grow weaker and weaker with each treatment and I knew on the inside that those treatments would kill him. I remember telling him he could opt to quit the treatments and enjoy his life. A few weeks later he told me he wasn't going back for the treatments. I watched him get stronger and stronger as the weeks went by and I knew he had made the right decision. He was

Introduction

still left with the nephrostomy bag that had to be replaced every three months through a short-procedure surgery. It also changed his entire life because he could never get a full night's sleep because he had to empty the bag every four to five hours. I learned so much from watching my dad go through that part of his life. I knew I could never complain about anything when this man smiled through all his challenges.

After the chemotherapy treatments, I realized I needed to move my dad in with me. I knew him and we had a bond where I knew when he was sick without him saying a word. Life was good from 2008 all the way up to December 31, 2014. It was New Year's Eve and my son and I left for church while my dad was in the kitchen eating. We returned home around 1 a.m. and the house was quiet. After a few minutes, my son said, "Something isn't right." He called for Pop-Pop and my dad answered with slurred speech. We ran in his room and he was slouched over the left side of the chair. He was saying, "Give me some Tylenol." I responded, "You need more than Tylenol; you had a stroke." I called 911 and they arrived within five minutes. My dad made us laugh the entire time, but I knew it was bad because we didn't know how long he had been in that state. Time is crucial with a stroke; you need treatment immediately in order to reduce the damage to the brain. They evaluated him and the diagnosis was serious, so they transferred him to a hospital that specialized in neuroscience and placed him in the intensive care unit. By this time his speech had cleared up but they told me he had paralysis on his left side and he would probably never walk again. I was devastated; I knew I could not take care of him by myself, so there was a chance he would have to go to a nursing home for care. The doctors later became confident that therapy would help him to get around and be partially independent. We admitted him to the rehabilitation hospital where he made progress.

Then one day I received a call that they were rushing him to the ER due to very low iron levels. When he was discharged from the hospital, they had downgraded his prognosis. He would spend the rest of his life in a wheelchair. The staff hoped to teach my dad to maneuver in the chair enough to be able to return home. In March 2015, I made the decision to bring my dad home because I was so frustrated with the care he was receiving in the rehabilitation centers and I was scared they were abusing or neglecting my dad. I would ask him questions about the happenings at the center but he wouldn't answer because he knew I would go off on the staff. My family decided we would all chip in to take care of Pop-Pop.

We spent the next few months taking care of my dad. We tried to get him to walk but he was so resistant to the physical therapist and occupational therapist. We had some of the funniest times together with my dad as we cared for him. We also had some of the most challenging times. My dad did not sleep well at night, so he would ring his bell at all times of the night whether or not he needed anything. At first it was funny but by the second month of sleep deprivation we all wanted to strangle him. He made us laugh and he made

INTRODUCTION

us cry. By July, all of us were exhausted and our backs hurt from lifting him in and out of the wheelchair, to and from bed. My dad was about 6'2" and 170 lbs. In August 2015, I had to make the toughest decision of my life. I had to put my dad in a nursing home. We found the perfect place right down the street from my sister's home. My sister went to see my dad twice a day and I went just about every day. My nieces and nephew all had their day to visit and we all went on Sundays. Dad was getting progressively worse; they could not keep his hemoglobin levels up. We all knew that he was not happy.

On Tuesday, March 3, 2015, I received a call from the nursing home that they were sending my dad to the hospital for a possible infection. I remember being so frustrated because I was tired of sitting in the ER every week. Besides that fact, when I left my dad at 8 p.m. the night before he was fine. When I got to the hospital my dad was lying in the bed and he looked fine, but my gut told me something was different this time. We sat there waiting for the blood work. They finally confirmed he had sepsis, a dangerous infection of the bloodstream. The doctors seemed really concerned, but I wasn't because he had had sepsis before. They started him on IV fluids and he began to holler about pain in his stomach. Then I noticed he had two bags of IV fluid and his nephrostomy bag was empty, his kidney was not draining. They prepped him to have the tube replaced. As we sat there waiting for the procedure, he started shaking.

I went over and covered him up and rubbed his hand and

he squeezed my hand. It was at that moment that I knew things were different. My dad never let us rub or hold his hand; he would always say, "Get off me." When he let me hold his hand I instantly knew something was different. He let me rub his forehead and I assured him it was OK for him to go home if he was tired. I let him know that I was OK and everyone would be fine. A few minutes later the blood pressure monitor went crazy. His blood pressure shot up to 215/89 and I looked at the monitor and snapped a picture and just as suddenly it went to 79/89. I called for the nurse and he looked at me then looked at the machine and back at me. He tried to get another reading but the machine stopped working. He had to go get a manual blood pressure monitor. Each reading still showed 79/89.

I saw the concern on the nurse's face and asked if a normal person would be panicking right now. He shook his head yes. I let him know that I understood what was happening and that I was OK. He nodded OK and then I went to get the doctor so they could get the procedure done for my dad. Now when the doctor returned to verify my dad's information, my dad just stared at us and would not answer so we took that as a sign of his decline. They did the procedure but his blood pressure was still the same. He was talking to me and the doctors didn't know what was going on. A specialist came in and told me they would give him medication that would immediately bring his blood pressure back up and they would place him in the ICU overnight so he could be better observed while on this medicine. I signed the papers, went to the ICU and when I left my dad he looked normal but his blood pressure was still low. He was talking to the nurses and seemed well. The crazy thing about this day was that I never updated my family on my dad's status and no one really called to ask. I sent a message when I got home letting them know that he would be staying in the hospital and then shared all the details.

I got up the next morning to go to see him. As I got off of the hospital elevator I could hear my dad yelling, "Help!" I wasn't nervous because this was normal for him, but as I got closer to the room, I knew something was wrong. There was a group of doctors near his room talking. I asked them if they were there for Mr. Pinkney and they said yes. I asked them how he was and they told me that his blood pressure was not responding to the medicine and he had not released any urine. His kidneys were failing. I went into the room to try to calm my dad but nothing worked this time. He kept saying, "June, help me." I told him I was going to get help. I went out and asked the doctor to give him pain medicine. The doctor said pain medicine lowers your blood pressure, and to give him that, they would have to stop the other medicine and he would pass shortly thereafter. I was not prepared for that. I told them we definitely wanted him to be pain-free but I needed time for my family to get a chance to come see him first. I went back in the room and told my dad I would be right back and help was on the way. I barely made it to the elevator and tears began to fall as I called my family to tell them the news. Everyone was coming to say bye to Pop-Pop. I remember sitting in the lobby crying as I talked to two close friends on the phone and they said they were coming to be with me. I had to get myself together to go back and take care of my dad.

As family and friends began to arrive, we tried to keep my dad comfortable and allow him to be awake so my sister, nieces and nephews could see him and talk to him one last time. My two nieces were able to see my dad and talk to him, but by the time the rest of the family arrived he was asleep because they had had to increase the dose of the pain medication because he was in so much pain. We all gathered around my dad and prayed for him and then they removed him from all the machines. At that moment, I lost it. I could not imagine what I would do without my dad. My dad was the only person that truly understood me.

For the first time in my life, I forgot about everyone and I began to cry and grieve for my dad. I was so grateful that my son was not there to see me break down that way. After I got myself together, they went back to check on my dad and he was still hanging on. The nurse told us that my dad would not pass with us watching him; she said he was too strong of a man to allow that. We decided to leave and they promised to call me if anything changed. I received a call around 2 a.m. that my dad was still hanging on and that they had to transfer him from the ICU to a regular room but they would make sure he remained comfortable.

My son was at college in California and he flew in expecting that my dad would have passed before he arrived the next morning but my dad was still alive. We could not make it to the hospital because there was a blizzard. I kept calling and checking on my dad all day but he was still fighting. The next day, which was two days after they told me he would pass immediately, we all went to see my dad. He was definitely transitioning but he was still fighting. My son was able to see his Pop-Pop one last time. The next day, when I went to go see him I knew he would not make it another day. Later that evening right after we got home they called to tell me my best friend was gone. I was numb and had to be strong for my family.

As we made plans for the funeral, I advised my family that I was doing my dad's eulogy. We decided to make his service a celebration and that it was. I do not remember what I said at the service but I know that family members who never go to church or with whom I rarely speak, came up to me and told me how my words affected their lives. My dad was truly an amazing man, father and grandfather. My life will never be the same without him. He did not leave us with a financial inheritance but he left us with words of wisdom, a sound work ethic and so many funny memories.

LIFT Yourself

LIFT Yourself 21-day Challenge

From the outside, it may look like you are living your dream life. You have a good job, a happy family, nice clothes and good friends. What more could a woman ask for? On the inside you are grateful for all that you have and all the things that you have helped people accomplish, yet you have this sense that life has more in store for you. For some, it is that desire to go back to get a degree even though you landed your dream job without it. For others it is the longing to start a business that is hampered by the fear of giving up a good job or comfortable lifestyle. And for others it is just a simple tug in your spirit yearning for you to put yourself first for a change instead of tending to the needs of everyone else.

The LIFT Yourself 21-day Challenge is designed to stir up that burning desire to live the fulfilled life you desire. It is meant to awaken the "little girl" in you who used to dream and fantasize about the way her life would be when she grew up. It is designed to stir up your imagination to all of the possibilities that await you if you unleash those dreams and passions that have been suppressed under the burdens and obligations of daily life. I believe that before you can LIFT anyone else, you must LIFT yourself.

Day 1

CHALLENGE: BE STILL

Women have a tendency to try to be all things to everyone and leave only the remnants for themselves. We are constantly running around meeting the demands of our jobs, the needs of our family and spending the rest of our time volunteering and saving the world. If you really want to be the best you, do the thing that is hardest — be still. I know, you think I am crazy. How can you find the time to be still when there are already not enough hours in the day to complete all the things that need to be done? Let me tell you a secret: by spending 15 minutes being still before you start your day, you will receive exponential growth in productivity. Men have long since mastered this concept; I think they hide out in the bathroom sometimes. They need to escape from the world.

In your quiet time find that center of peace that you once had before you became everything to everyone. If you never experienced that peace, it is something you need to tap into. Give yourself 15 minutes to be selfish; do not think of anyone but yourself. Tap into the things that you need to do for yourself. Tap into that inner place of refuge where you are safe from judgments, where you no longer care what people think about you or your decisions. Tap into that place where you can dream about the life that you believe you should have. Give yourself permission to fantasize and believe that life is possible.

Here are some questions to ask yourself as you reflect.

What do you like to do when you are alone?

....
....
....

What are some of the promises that you make to yourself?

....
....
....

What are some of the things you say to yourself frequently?

....
....
....

Tap into the things that you need to do for yourself.

Day 2

CHALLENGE: BE TRUE TO YOURSELF

Excerpt from my journal dated Jan. 18, 2000 - during the time of my dad's initial illness

I am free. Free to think, free to love, free to receive love, free to talk, free to listen. Free to agree or disagree. Free to forgive. I am truly grateful for this day and this time in my life. I am cutting all ties to the past. In my past I had low self-esteem, I didn't speak my mind because I wanted to keep the peace. From this point on I will pray to God and then speak my peace. I have suffered heartache in the past but now I am ready to forgive and forget. I am open to love and ready to give love like never before. I am truly grateful to God for the way he is shaping my mind. I now truly feel that if I can seek God, I can truly be happy. No longer worried about how people feel about me. I spent my life trying to please my parents and trying to fit in with my friends.

In the solitude of your mind are the answers to all your questions about life. You must take the time to ask and listen.

What do I want to do with my life?

....
....
....

What is my purpose for living?

....
....
....

What are my gifts and strengths?

....
....
....

What are my weaknesses and how can I develop them into strengths?

....
....
....

Day 3

CHALLENGE: BE HAPPY

Give yourself permission to be happy. Be happy in spite of whatever is going on in your life. Be happy that you are alive. Be happy that you were chosen to encounter every situation that you have experienced. Be happy that you survived situations that people don't even know about. Be happy that you were chosen for greatness. Be happy that you will be able to assist others in achieving their greatness. Be happy that someone helped you reach your level of greatness. Be happy that as we all travel our roads to greatness, we will be able to impact each other.

Happiness has been the topic of many conversations that I have had lately with women in my professional circle and in my circle of friends, most of them in their late 30s. Collectively, they have communicated how they sacrificed their own happiness to satisfy the needs of their spouses, children and parents. These women all expressed that they would have been so much more fulfilled in their relationships if they had realized the importance of making their personal goals and aspirations a priority.

What makes you happy?

....
....
....

What keeps you from being happy?

....
....
....

What are some reasons for you to celebrate yourself?

....
....
....
....

> *Give yourself permission to be happy.*

Day 4

CHALLENGE: NEVER LET CIRCUMSTANCES DEFINE YOU

I always struggled with identifying myself as a single mother. Yes, I had a baby out of wedlock but my son's dad was in his life. We made a pact with each other that even though we were not married we would raise our son together and that we would do everything we could to defy all the stereotypes of baby mama drama. We did an amazing job at this. There were many times when people would see us together with our son and assume that we were married and we would just look at each other and smile. We made sure we went to all school functions together if we were in town and not traveling. We were able to maintain a really close friendship because we did not let the stigma of having a baby out of wedlock negatively define our lives. We chose a different route than most single parents: co-parenting. We decided to make a new standard for dealing with something that was not ideal. I remember people looking at me strangely when I explained that my son's father and I got along well and that we actually liked each other. I would like to think that we made an impact on the people that knew us and saw how we were able to maneuver through difficult situations with class and precision.

Many times in our personal as well as professional lives,

circumstances are not the ideal, but we must make a conscious decision to deal with adversity as if they were the ideal situation. True leaders are able to take any situation and maneuver it to work in their favor. There will be times when you must develop a strategy to defy the odds, to stand out from the status quo. Be the leader in your own life, take charge of not-so-perfect situations with decisiveness and raw determination. In the process of turning things around, you likely will draw positive attention to yourself. Taking the road less traveled most likely will give you far greater exposure than responding in the normal way. Famous people are never lauded for maintaining the status quo; they earn their fame by taking risks or being different.

At the company I work for, the Chairman's award is given to an employee who does something to exemplify the company's core values while exceeding the expectations of their normal job duties. The recipients of this award are flown to Boston and treated like celebrities, meeting with the company president and enjoying extravagant dinners. These exceptional employees are recognized as the cream of the crop for an entire year. A reputation as a person committed to excellence is golden. Strive to create a personal brand that embodies the qualities of a Chairman's award winner.

Life will rarely present us with perfect conditions; our job is to create the ideal outcome from the circumstances in which we find ourselves. A great example of imperfection is family. People joke all the time that you can't choose your family, but you would if you could. Most of us love and create great memories with our families despite the fact that there is always one member that doesn't fit in or causes trouble; we still love them.

What situations have you faced in life that were less than ideal?

....
....
....

In what ways were you able to demonstrate leadership qualities in your response to the situations?

....
....
....

How would you handle a less-than-perfect situation as a leader?

....
....
....
....

Day 5

CHALLENGE: PURSUE PASSION

Passion has become a popular buzzword among many corporations. Some have jumped on the bandwagon of creating a passion statement because it sounds good and it makes the corporation look like they are really concerned about their employees working for a purpose greater than a paycheck. When I did some research to try to drive home the importance of finding your passion and living life on your own terms, the best definition I found came from an unlikely source. The online Urban Dictionary defines passion as "when you put more energy into something than is required to do it." Passion is ambition that materializes into action. In the corporate world, the more passion employees pour into their jobs, the greater the company's profit will be. The more you pursue your passion, the greater the benefits you will see in your life. Pursuing goals you are passionate about is non-negotiable. When your ambition is turned into action, a chain reaction is going to happen in your life. The more you see the fruits of your passion manifested into reality, the more passion will be ignited in you. Conversely, the more you settle for living in mediocrity, the less passion will burn in you. We all know that a woman operating in her passion is a magnet for making things happen. Passion leads to purpose.

Think back to your childhood.

What are some toys, clothing or other things you wish you kept from your younger days?

....
....
....
....

What are some places you would love to explore?

....
....
....
....
....
....

> *Passion is ambition that materializes into action.*

Day 6

CHALLENGE: EXPLORE, BUT HEED THE WARNING SIGNS

One day while I babysat my 3-year-old nephew he found two umbrellas, one of which would not close properly. I explained to him that it was broken and that he should not play with it. He obeyed me and put it down. The second one was a compact, black umbrella with colorful polka dots. He walked around the house with the umbrella for hours saying, "umbrella." I was intrigued by how something so simple could entertain him for such a long time. Then he figured out how to extend the handle and was trying to push it in to close it. I knew if he wasn't careful he would smash his fingers, so I repeatedly said, "Be careful," and he repeated my words. I asked him to bring me the umbrella before he got hurt but he didn't listen and almost hurt his hand. The thing is, the baby could not see the possibility of getting hurt from something that was bringing him so much joy. But I knew from experience that the umbrella that provided protection could also cause pain. We as adults are the same way, we find ourselves in situations that we know are not in our best interest but we continue to hang around until we get hurt and then we run for safety. We have to learn to explore more and listen to the signs that warn us of impending danger.

What are some times that you knew the thing that looked good was definitely dangerous?

....
....
....
....

How would things have been different if you had heeded the warning signs?

....
....
....

What lesson(s) did you learn from those experiences?

....
....
....

> *Listen to the signs that warn of impending danger.*

Day 7

CHALLENGE: NEVER TAKE NO FOR AN ANSWER

Let's learn from the children in our lives. Let's embrace the possibilities and not let anyone keep us from pursuing our dreams.

If you've ever cared for a toddler, you know their most popular word is *no*. As I prepared my nephew for naptime, I said "Get in the bed," and "Let's take a nap," and the response was an almost silent "no." I didn't get mad because after all this was not my child, so the comment was cute and not disrespectful. However, after 10 minutes of him moving around on the bed with no intention of taking a nap, I went out of the room for a minute. By the time I returened, he had climbed out of bed and was playing. I repeatedly shouted, "No playing; get in the bed!" No matter how many times I said no, he continued to do what he wanted to do. This made me chuckle on the inside because I knew that if I faced my obstacles in life with the same persistence I would be unstoppable.

What would you do if you knew that you only had one week left to live?

....
....
....
....

What are some of your fears?

....
....
....

What would you do if you knew you could not fail?

....
....
....

> *Let's embrace the possibilities and not let anyone keep us from pursuing our dreams.*

Day 8

CHALLENGE: BALANCE

There is an exercise we do at my gym where you stand on one leg and lean forward with your arms outstretched and all your weight balanced on one leg. Whenever people start to lose their balance, the instructor tells us to focus on a specific object and we will regain our balance. Every time I started to lose my balance, I focused on an object in the front of the room and I regained my balance. This demonstration made me think about how in life there are times of imbalance when I feel the weight of the world on my shoulders. Those are usually the times when my brain is overloaded and I am not focused. It helps me to remember this exercise and what it will take to regain balance.

What are some times when you have felt most out of balance?

....
....
....

How did you recover?

....
....
....

What advice would you give to someone in the same situation?

....
....
....

Get focused and regain your balance.

Day 9

CHALLENGE: VULNERABILITY

Confident women lift each other up. I have often heard that women do not support each other enough. I want to contribute to changing that image of women. I envision a world where women are able to support and lift each other without fearing it will make them miss out on opportunities. The Bible states in Luke 6:38, "Give, and it will be given unto you. A good measure, pressed down, shaken together and running over, will be poured into your lap. For with the measure you use, it will be measured to you." This is the image I want you to have when you think of lifting up women that you encounter.

You may be wondering what vulnerability and confidence have to do with each other. Vulnerability is opening yourself up to the risk of being hurt or harmed. Humans are naturally selfish and our natural instinct is to protect ourselves. In order to lift someone up, you have to be willing to risk that they may end up in a higher position than you. Dealing with this reality will require a great level of vulnerability and selflessness. When you think of the Scripture reference, you won't worry about the person surpassing you because you know that when you uplift someone there will also be someone who will be there for you when you need to be lifted. The LIFT Yourself 21-day Challenge is designed to encourage conversations among women in which they share their successes, failures and trials with each other. This openness will help women get to the place in life where they are operating from their core values and maximizing their gifts and talents.

The Mary Kay cosmetics company and its beauty consultants demonstrate this principle at its finest. At my first Mary Kay sales meeting, I entered the room and it was filled with beautiful well-dressed women who were smiling, laughing, hugging and joking. As the meeting went on, we got to the portion where they did a sales round-up where everyone disclosed their prior week's sales amount. I was amazed as every woman in the room applauded and cheered for each other. This was very strange to me because in the corporate world, you do not cheer for your competition when they have higher sales totals than you. Mary Kay cosmetics demonstrates that when women lift each other up we all succeed. There is really no competition in these meetings because there is room for everyone at the top. Everyone shares their sales tactics and techniques because they want each person to have an opportunity to be successful. I wish every woman could experience the feeling of being in a group of women where everyone is vulnerable yet confident enough to lift each other up to experience success.

When have you benefited from another woman lifting you up?

....
....
....

How can you incorporate uplifting other women into your life?

....
....
....

What do you see as the link between confidence and vulnerability?

....
....
....

Confident women lift each other up.

Day 10

CHALLENGE: SELF WORTH

Excerpt from my journal dated Jan. 21, 2000 – during my dad's initial illness

As I look back over my life, I am rather disappointed in myself. Somewhere along the line I laid down my true self and began living a lie. I began to settle for mediocrity when all my life I had strived for the best. When I graduated from high school, I graduated at the top of my class and was accepted to the best universities. But at some point over the last 7 years I forgot who I was and what I wanted from life. I am tired of living in poverty. I am tired of struggling with money, and I am tired of being angry with people. I am tired of saying I want better but just sitting back and not going to get it. From this moment on I am reclaiming my old self, the person who relentlessly pursued her dreams. I am determined to get out of debt and out of poverty. I am going to give my son that which I did not have. I am going to show my nieces that they do not have to settle in life; they can have whatever they are willing to work for. I am going to get body and mind together. I am going to let God have his way in my life. I am setting goals.

I then listed my short-term goals, which I accomplished within 12 months.

Short-term goals:

- *Get a new car.* I had an old car that was constantly breaking down and in need of repairs. The unexpected expenses prevented me from sticking to my budget. My dad told me to get a reliable car with a car note that would fit in my budget.
- *Pay off two bills.*
- *Start looking for a house to purchase.* I wanted to buy a house so that I could stop renting. Purchasing a home would allow me to build equity as well as take advantage of tax breaks that were available to homeowners.

I also wrote out my big-picture values that would guide my life-long decisions.

- *Be obedient to God.*
- *Be true to myself.*
- *Live within my means*
- *Save for the future*

What are your goals?

Short-term goals:

....

....

....

....

What values will guide your future decisions?

....

....

....

....

> *You can have whatever you are willing to work for.*

Day 11

CHALLENGE: VISION

If you truly want to LIFT yourself, you must make up your mind to become an effective leader of your life. To make the greatest progress in your life, you must resolve to become the CEO of your life. If you think of your life as an organization and you are the one in charge of every outcome, then you start to operate more effectively. In an organization, the CEO's primary responsibility is setting the vision.

For many years, I floated through life, sometimes with goals and sometimes just reacting to whatever life threw at me. Most of the time I knew I wasn't living up to my full potential even though I looked pretty successful by society's standards. I had a very successful accounting career for a major insurance company and I was able to maneuver my way up the corporate ladder. Then one day it hit me. As I sat in a room full of new managers for a training session with top executives in our company, I realized I could be so much more successful if I implemented the company's leadership strategies in my own life.

Vision was the central topic of the training. The executives were very clear about the vision of our company, and their task was to instill that vision in the management team so that we could effectively convey it to our team members. As an employee, I was only vaguely familiar with the company's vision and never really thought that it had much to do with me because I wasn't in management until now. As a new manager, I quickly realized that the level of success that my team achieved was directly related to how well I communicated the vision for the company and for our team.

Once I understood the impact of a clearly defined vision on the success of an organization, I started evaluating my own life. I had read many, many books that talked about creating a vision for your life and I had attempted to map it out on paper numerous times without much success. Now I had the knowledge I needed to articulate my vision for my personal life. Rather than just reacting to situations according to how I felt that day, I was now forced to examine each situation based on how it would impact the vision I had created for my life.

In your daydreams, what does your ideal life look like?

....

....

....

....

....

....

....

What is your vision for your future?

....
....
....
....
....
....

What steps will you take to achieve the vision?

....
....
....
....
....
....

Become an effective leader of your life.

Day 12

CHALLENGE: BELIEVE

In the last 20 years of his life, my dad had posted index cards all around his room with Scriptures and various quotes that reminded him to keep his thoughts positive. We used to tease him about his cards, because he was a horrible speller and the way he wrote the quotes was hilarious to us. The magical thing is, it didn't matter how he spelled the words. The fact that he wrote things down and was constantly viewing them throughout his day was life changing for him. I had no idea how powerful this little act was until he passed away and I was going through his things. He had notes everywhere, in his wallet, in his dresser, on his nightstand, taped to his mirror and TV. The powerful part of these cards is that they helped my dad live through a host of major illnesses that could have killed him years before he died.

His doctors would often stand in amazement as we listed all the major things he had wrong with him yet he was still a vibrant character up until he turned 79. The secret to overcoming his physical condition was his positive state of mind. My dad never talked about having cancer and one kidney and heart problems, he just went to the doctors, took the treatments, exercised and tried to lived his life as normally as he could. In order to avoid having to recite his illnesses to the doctors, he wrote all his conditions, surgeries and medications on a sheet of paper and handed it to the doctor to update his file.

When I first saw him do this, I thought it was just a smart idea and a timesaver. However, after I witnessed my dad's positive attitude during his sickness I realized why he made up the list in the first place. The more you repeat your negative circumstances, the more power they continue to have. My dad was smart enough to understand that if you feed your mind positive thoughts, you can overcome any obstacle that comes your way. I know that positive thought training had saved my dad's life quite a few times when he had so many close calls.

I previously told you my dad suffered a major stroke that left him in a wheelchair. While he was in the rehabilitation center, he received a mental capacity test after the stroke and due to his age he also was tested for dementia. The therapist that gave my dad the mental capacity test was blown away at his ability to calculate math and sequences at a speed faster than both she and I could. And he was an 80-year-old stroke patient! When she finished, she just looked in amazement and told him his mental capacity was amazing and he did not need treatment from her. She also stated that she hoped her mind was that sharp when she was his age. This experience had a major impact on my life. At that point I realized that my dad had demonstrated the power of training your mind to think and stay positive. I was fortunate enough to inherit the stack of index cards with my dad's motivational quotes on them and they have inspired me to share with everyone that there is truth in the idea that changing your thoughts will change your life.

I shared the inspiring notecards with several of my co-workers and one reported back to me a few months later that she had started posting notes to herself, on her bathroom mirror and her computer monitor. She wanted to keep her mind filled with positive affirmations and to keep her goals in the forefront of her mind. She admitted that she had heard the importance of making this a practice, but when I told her the impact this practice had on my dad she was inspired to put it into action. She was elated to report to me that she had seen a dramatic change in her outlook on life and the way she responded to situations as a result of keeping her mind focused on staying positive.

What are the qualities you like most about yourself?

....
....
....

What are some things you say to yourself daily?

....
....
....

Write out three positive affirmations for yourself and repeat them daily.

1. ....
....
....

2. ....
....
....

3. ....
....
....

" *Changing your thoughts will change your life.*

Day 13

CHALLENGE: SURRENDER

Surrender and submit are two powerful words, but for many women they are also horrible words. These words require us to relinquish control of our lives and require us to be vulnerable to the actions of God or another person. These concepts also can be liberating when we learn to put down the title of Superwoman and just let go.

I worked with a young lady who was a new mom. She started a new job that had dramatically more responsibilities than her previous job. During our initial conversations she assured me that she was just fine handling her new duties. She stated she had a plan in place for childcare and she just needed to adjust to her new position. As the weeks went on, she began to lose her enthusiasm and pure exhaustion set in. I sat down with her and asked her a series of questions about her daily routine. As she answered my questions, she admitted that she was overwhelmed and did not know what to do. We mapped out all her daily and weekly duties and indicated areas where she could seek assistance and get some relief. Initially, the idea of asking others for assistance did not sit well with her.

Once I explained to her that getting assistance would

provide her more time to do the things that mattered the most, like spend time with her family, she agreed that there were tasks that she could delegate. Before the tasks could be delegated, she had to document the entire job that she wanted someone else to handle. In the end, she reported back to me that the time and energy spent documenting the tasks was worth it and freed her to tend to her family and personal needs.

The battle to surrender is tough but rewarding when we learn to release our fears and reservations. Some people are stuck in an unhealthy cycle because they have not submitted to the dreams that are buried inside of them. A woman that learns to surrender and submit to the plans that God has for her, is a woman on a quest to find her higher calling in life. She is a woman who has discovered the art of self-denial.

One of the most important things that you need is to surrender your past failures or disappointments. Whatever it is that you started and did not complete, or whatever plan you had that did not turn out the way you envisioned it, release it. Take a deep a breath in and let it out slowly. This is an exercise you will need to practice as you recall every broken promise to yourself.

You probably did not even realize the impact those events had on keeping you from currently fulfilling your goals. I want you to release those feelings and embrace the joy and excitement that you will feel when you reach your goal.

Maybe you need to do more than breathe deeply in order to

release those feelings of regret. Let's go a step further. Grab a blank sheet of paper and a pen. Write a list of all the things that have not worked out as expected. When you're finished writing the list, fold it up so it fits in an envelope. Rip the paper in half and keep ripping it until it is unreadable and until you feel better.

There are two benefits of the exercise:

1. Writing your thoughts frees your mind.

2. Ripping the paper destroys the words you wrote and provides a stress reliever.

Submit to the dreams buried inside of you.

Day 14

CHALLENGE: BE COURAGEOUS

I had always dreamed of moving from Philadelphia to Atlanta. This was a dream of mine long before Atlanta became the hotspot for young urban professionals. Once I had my son I knew my dream would not become a reality because my son needed to be around his family. But one day I was discussing my dream of moving to Atlanta with a girlfriend, and she shared the same desire to move there. The only difference was she did not have any children. We began to talk and look at places there, and eventually we planned a trip to visit Atlanta to see if we really liked it. Throughout our planning, I knew that moving was not a possibility for me for a few more years until my son was off to college. He was almost 10 at the time. When I visited the city I instantly fell in love with it and my desire to relocate there was heightened.

I came back from the trip and began to evaluate everything in my life and I realized that the move would be a perfect chance for me to start over and to live my life for myself. I knew that my son would be fine adjusting to the move. People moved with their children all the time. I was financially prepared to make a move and I decided that I was going to live for me and do what felt right for me instead of playing things safe.

I was able to find a place to live that was very affordable and much nicer than I could ever afford in Philadelphia. When I announced my decision to my family, no one took me seriously. I made the announcement in October that I was going to move at the end of December so my son could start his new school after Christmas break. People did not take me seriously until I started coming home every night and packing up our belongings. The person that took the news the hardest was my son's dad. He did not want me to move his son away from him, but I had to do what felt right for me. At the time he was traveling a lot so he could come visit us. I resigned from my job in November and we moved to Atlanta on December 29, 2004.

Looking back, that was the best decision that I ever made in my life. I stepped out on faith and did what I wanted to do for the first time in my life. We had some of the best times during our short stay in Atlanta. I did not work during that time so I was able to take and pick up my son to and from school everyday and have lunch with him some days. We spent a lot of time talking and playing, things I did not have time to do in Philadelphia, where I was working and catering to the needs of everyone in my family. My son and I only stayed in Atlanta until the end of the school year because he had a really hard time adjusting to life without his dad and the rest of his family. While we were enjoying our time together in our new city, he yearned for the interaction with his other family members. We learned that you could do whatever you want in life as long as you have a plan and some courage. I was able to pick up and move in a little under two months and I never looked back to worry about how people felt about my decision. When I moved back they never received an explanation either, because during that experience I learned to live life on my own terms.

I struggled with the decision to move back to Philadelphia because I really wanted to build a new life for my son and myself. I battled inwardly with my own selfish desires and the best interest of my son. My motherly nature won and I decided to move back to Philadelphia. I remember when I made this decision to move back, my dad and my son's father were very excited. My son started counting down the days until he could see his Pop-Pop again. It was at that point that I realized that being a mom meant that I would have to sacrifice my own desires until my son became an adult.

My friend kept asking me what I was going to say when people asked me why I came back, and honestly I wasn't going to respond because I knew that I was doing the best thing for my son and me. In my mind, I didn't owe anyone an explanation. Fortunately for me, I have a strong personality so no one really asked me any questions about moving back. However, there was no denying that my hiatus in Atlanta was exactly what I needed. I came back clear headed and very determined to live life on my own terms. When I returned, I did not immediately get a job so people did start insinuating that I needed to work. But I did not care what they thought. I had enough financial resources to take care of my expenses. I was determined to find a job that I wanted to work, not a job that I needed to work. After two months I was able to secure a new job that fulfilled many of my requirements.

In retrospect, if I had the chance to go back in time, I would definitely make the decision to move again. I have had conversations with my son about the move now that he is older. Though he had some struggles as a result of our move, he also agrees that the lessons outweigh the regrets. We learned that you could do whatever you want in life as long as you have a plan and some courage. When it came time for my son to go to college, many of his friends were apprehensive about leaving their hometown, but he applied to colleges all over the country knowing there was more to life than Philadelphia.

Courage is the ability to do something that you know is difficult. What are some things that you always wanted to do but fear stopped you?

....

....

....

....

....

If you had the opportunity to move anywhere you wanted where would it be?

....

....

....

What does courageous look like to you?

....

....

....

Make a plan and have courage.

Day 15

CHALLENGE: LEAD

I was recently at a seminar on work/life balance with the head of Human Resources for a major corporation. She was asked how she manages to balance the demands of an executive position as a mother and wife. She responded that she is the CEO of an organization and she is the CEO of her life. She manages her personal life the same way she manages her corporate life. She has calendars, schedules and she gets help when she needs to. That was her way of handling her many obligations, although she noted that not all women are wired to manage their affairs the same way.

As I listened to her remarks, I was relieved and felt a sense of joy because that was how I approached my life—in a very business-minded way.

In order to LIFT ourselves to a new place in life, we have to learn to manage our lives as the CEO. When I think back to the times in my life when I was the busiest, those were the times I accomplished the most.

When I finally decided to finish my bachelor's degree by taking classes on campus, it was as if all hell broke loose to keep me from achieving that goal. I remember my son was in elementary school and he had a lot of homework each night because he attended private school.

His father and I had worked out an arrangement that he would pick him up from school each Monday so that I could attend class and he would bring him to my dad's house when it was time for him to go to bed. All went well for the first few weeks. Then I would come home at night thinking everything was fine, only to wake up the next morning to find my son in tears because his homework wasn't done. We would scramble to get it done before dashing out to school and work at 7 a.m. I remember telling myself that this was only temporary; I only had one year of school left.

Then the bottom fell out. My son's dad started traveling more, and of course he was always gone on the one day I needed him, Mondays. My dad was available to keep my son but there was one problem, he didn't drive and my son's school was a 30-minute car drive or an hour bus ride away from my house. I had to figure something out because postponing my degree again was not an option. After analyzing everything, I decided my only choice was to work part-time so that I could leave work and drive 30 minutes to my son's school and then 30 minutes home to drop my son off at my dad's, then take the 40-minute commute to school.

Many did not understand how I could afford to work part-time and why I was doing all that driving just to get a degree. But to me, it was much bigger than getting a degree. First off, I barely had time but I made that sacrifice because I needed to finish the degree I had started almost 10 years prior. Second, I needed to be able to tell my son later in life that there is no excuse not to achieve your goals. There is always a way, albeit expensive and time-consuming, but nonetheless there is a way.

That time in my life was one of my most productive because I had to develop a plan to make it all work. My schedule was full—I worked 32 hours a week, went to school on Mondays from 5 to 9 p.m., attended church on Tuesday and Thursday evenings and squeezed in homework, raising my son, and tending to our household. I felt fulfilled.

I developed a meal prep schedule because I did not want my dad to have to cook meals for my son on the days he was watching him; that was my obligation. So after church on Sunday I would wash our clothes and prepare meals for Sunday, Monday and Tuesday. Then on Wednesday I would prepare meals for that day and Thursday.

We ordered take out or ate leftovers on the weekends. I became very regimented and tried to teach my son a regimen, but he was not so cooperative. All my planning helped cut down on the stress of him being a free spirit. I remember the day I graduated, my son and my dad were there and I was so happy because I was able to show that you can achieve anything you put your mind to if you are determined.

It also was important to me that my son saw that I did not neglect my relationship with God while I was achieving my goal. l never neglected the three days a week of church services during that year of completing my degree. I remember my son was so happy when I was finished with school. We kept up the schedules that we implemented during that time because it gave us order and structure, and it allowed me more time to spend talking, laughing and playing with my son.

Are you acting as the CEO of your life?

....

....

....

What areas do you need to manage better?

....

....

....

List some times where you depended on people and they let you down? What did you do to handle being let down?

....

....

....

Day 16

CHALLENGE: INCORPORATE

As women, we often feel like we have to do everything ourselves. But failure to incorporate others into your plans and strategies for achieving your goals will hinder you from achieving your vision.

Are there certain people who are key to implementing your goals and strategies for your life? Which individuals will comprise your support system? You're probably thinking, "I already have a support system" or "I don't need a support system; I cannot depend on other people." Let me tell you, I was that woman also.

One of the primary groups of stakeholders in a corporation is the board of directors; they are responsible for protecting the interests of shareholders. In this step, I am asking you to build a board of directors for your life. These people will be responsible for protecting you and making sure you accomplish your goals. This network will include mentors, coaches and your childcare/eldercare network.

Mothers often neglect self-care and put off pursuing their personal goals because they place the needs of their children and family before their own. This is a mother's natural instinct, but you have to remember that you cannot pour from an empty container.

When your children are young, you want to be there so you can witness every milestone. Then as they get older, you're dashing from work to pick up the children. Life between work and home becomes a taxi service of dropping the kids off at after-school activities along with attending parent teacher conferences, back-to-school night, PTA meetings and the list could go on forever. Most moms are burned out by the time they get home after all those activities, but there is no time to be tired because the kids still need to eat, do homework, and get bathed; and moms need to try squeezing in some quality time for themselves.

In hindsight, I realize that I would have been so much more productive as a mom if I had incorporated the assistance of people around me a little more. Trying to be Supermom did not make me a great mom, it made me a tired, cranky mom. I remember a time when my son was in elementary school and I was forced to get a family friend to pick up my son from school for a few months. I felt terrible at first that I needed to get help in taking care of my son. However, what I realized after a few days was that my son and the family friend were having a great time together. When I picked him up, he would be in the best mood because he had had an after school snack. My friend even sent him home with a home-cooked meal some days. The most remarkable thing was that our ride home and our evening routine went so much smoother because my son was happy and I was relaxed because I knew that some of the tasks that I needed to complete were already taken care of. My son is in college now and he still talks about the memories he had during that period of his life. I encourage mothers to drop your pride and reach out to others for assistance with some of the tasks you think you need to complete yourself.

On a scale of 1 to 10, how willing are you to ask for help?

....

What prevents you from asking for help?

....

....

....

What tasks can you get assistance to help complete?

....

....

....

" *You cannot pour from an empty container.*

Day 17

CHALLENGE: FOLLOW THROUGH

You promised yourself you were going to take some time for yourself each week but unfortunately that has not happened. You promised yourself you would start working out, eating healthier or maybe going back to school to get that degree. You got so busy with everyone else that you never got around to fulfilling those promises.

Every time you make a promise to yourself and then fail to follow through, you are letting yourself off the hook and killing your determination. Before you know it, you are letting yourself off the hook for more and more things. This slowly eats away at your self-esteem, which then allows you to more easily place the needs of everyone above your own needs.

Before you know it, you exist to meet the needs of everyone else because you have undermined the value of your needs. I am not telling you something I heard. I am telling you what I experienced. I just never realized this was happening until I found myself living a very chaotic life, where I had once lived as a very, very organized person. I sat back and starting reflecting on how I got from the organized, neat person to the person that lacked order and clarity.

I remembered that it started at a point where I was very busy in life, and I had started letting things that were important to me slide so that I could fulfill other obligations. Most of those obligations were helping other people. It was little things, like not putting my shoes back where they belonged when I took them off, and leaving them on the bedroom floor instead. Now this may seem trivial to some but having everything in its proper place was very important to me. When I did not hold myself accountable to a very small promise, I was telling myself it was OK to let other things slide.

But what happened was that practice of letting myself off the hook for small things began to trickle over to other areas of my life. When I didn't feel like exercising or reading a book, I just convinced myself that it was OK to skip those tasks because I was tired or busy. Within a few years, I was very disorganized. I wasn't working out and I had not finished reading a book in over a year. I had started reading lots of books but finished none. When I was the person that kept every promise I made to myself, I was organized, happy and making major accomplishments. Discipline is developed through consistency.

What are some things you can do to become more disciplined?

....

....

....
....

What are the top three things you want to do for yourself?

....
....
....

What prevents you from doing the things you need to do?

....
....
....

How would your life look if you kept your promises to yourself?

....
....
....

> *Letting yourself off the hook will eat away at your self-esteem.*

Day 18

CHALLENGE: TRAIN

They say the road to success is a lonely journey. I understand this more and more each day. It is not that people don't support you or encourage you. The loneliness comes in battling the distractions and the attacks that are trying their best to get you to quit before you reach your goal. It is during the times that you are just about to quit or take a break that something will happen to remind you of your passion. If there is no passion behind what you are doing, it is easy to abort the mission. You have to train yourself to focus on the end result. I have seen many people start out on a journey to return to school and pursue a degree because they want to earn more money at their job. The thing they fail to realize is that often the desire for higher income doesn't compare to quality time with your family or the reward of completing a degree.

When I decided to go back to school to get my MBA, I didn't do it to get a better job, I wanted to demonstrate to my son and my nieces and nephews the importance of education and that is was possible for someone in our family to get an advanced degree. It was this passion that allowed me to sacrifice a majority of my free time to complete my coursework. I remember coming home each night from work, at that time my son was in junior high and I had my nephew who was in high school living with me. At first, they couldn't understand why I spent so many hours in front of my computer. As time went on and they saw that I was committed to my work, and they would join me in the living room as I worked on my computer. It became a sort of family time.

We would watch the same movie every Monday as I typed my paper. It was somewhere around the fourth month of watching the same movie that they questioned me as to why we watched this movie each week and I explained I knew the movie by heart so it allowed me to stay focused on my assignment. When I needed I a break, I could look up for a few minutes and then get back to work. I went on to explain that if I watched a new movie while working on my papers, I would get distracted and it would take me longer to complete my assignment. We began to make a joke about watching the same movie, but each week they knew where to find me. On most Mondays they were both with me while I worked. The thing that they did not realize was that having them sit with me while I worked helped fuel me with more passion to complete my degree during the times that I wanted to quit. I knew that I had two young men watching me and I was subconsciously instilling in them discipline and consistency.

If it was not for my passion to set an example for my family, I would have quit pursuing my MBA somewhere around the third class, because that was when the novelty of my decision wore off. Also at that time, my life became so busy that I did not have extra time to do anything but go to work and school. I have never been a quitter and when the odds are stacked against me, I go even harder to achieve my goal. This time, my determination was not just for me, it was for those that were watching me.

How have you trained yourself to push past obstacles?

....

....

....

List some times where you quit because the opposition was too great?

....

....

....

Name a time when you achieved your goals in spite of obstacles? What lessons did you learn?

....

....

....

Day 19

CHALLENGE: CONFIDENCE

My dad always told me, "Dress for the next position you want." At first I did not understand what he meant, because when I first started working I dressed really nice every day. But as time went on, I began to see that not everyone dressed up so I got comfortable dressing like everyone else. When I reached a plateau in my career, I remembered his advice. I started dressing up more and something magical happened. I started to feel better and that led to me being more confident in myself. That confidence caught the attention of my peers and leaders and I began to excel in my career. Now I can tell you from a 20-year career with many peaks and valleys in my work attire, there is a definite link between my appearance and appearing more confident, knowledgeable and career-minded.

When I decided to make a change in my life, it always started with changing the way I looked on the outside. Here are some ways you can make a small change on the outside that will give you confidence to make the steps necessary to reach your goals:

- Put some makeup on.

- Put on some heels or a nice pair of shoes.

- Add some accessories to your outfits.

- Get a new lipstick color.

Have you ever been invited to an event and you were not sure of the dress code? You picked out the outfit you thought was best only to get to the event and discover you were way overdressed/underdressed and you just wanted to disappear? You managed to find a seat and you tried to remain seated as much as possible so that people would not recognize your wardrobe mistake. I am glad I am not the only one that has ever done that!

Now picture this: you have been invited to a wedding and you are excited to go and determined to show up and show out for this event. You get the perfect dress, hottest shoes, get your hair, nails and makeup done. When you walk in the room you want all eyes on you and they are. All night people are complimenting you and you are making your rounds enjoying the attention. In both situations the only difference was your level of confidence in yourself. If you had had the confidence level from situation #2 in situation #1, the people would have responded favorably also because you embodied confidence. I want you to have the confidence to walk into any event and own the room even if you are not dressed like everyone else. Carry yourself like you intentionally chose to dress differently because you are a trendsetter and a leader in every situation.

What are some things you do to make yourself feel pretty?

....
....
....

List some activities you will use to shift your attitude on an imperfect day.

....
....
....

List some times when you exuded confidence and you felt great about it.

....
....
....

Dress for the next position you want.

Day 20

CHALLENGE: LOVE

Today I challenge you to think of a love relationship you have had that did not work out the way you wanted it to. Sit down and write that person a letter forgiving them for the failure of the relationship.

What was the love lesson that you learned from this relationship?

....
....
....

How will you incorporate this lesson into your life?

....
....
....

Day 21

CHALLENGE: PRAYER/MEDITATION

Prayer was essential to me in surviving my hard season. It is amazing how God will prepare you for your test before it begins. Prayer was birthed out of me in 2006. I was studying under a great woman of God and prayer warrior. She had me pray and would not let me stop until June ended and the Holy Spirit took over. I would pray at the beginning of service each week and God would just drop words into my mouth. I would pray until I had no physical strength but my spirit was free and doing the will of God. I prayed so much that it became who I was. I would talk to God throughout the day. When I realized that prayer was communication with God, I realized I was utilizing this gift fully. I needed some changes in my life, but I could not make them happen on my own. I figured I would try to get God involved. I started praying to God about everything. I prayed for him to show me how to dress, how to raise my son, how to handle my anger and manage my finances. I began to see situations in my life get better and if they didn't, I had more peace and less anger about them. God was answering my prayers and building my faith in Him. The only refuge I had from trouble was when I was praying. When I prayed, boldness would come over me. I would let God control me and I felt at peace.

As things began to get worse, I would just pray. I didn't pray for myself but for other people. I was dealing with the end of a relationship, my dad being sick, working full time and raising a young child. I remember days where I didn't even have time to eat because I was taking care of everyone else.

It was during that time that I started getting up earlier in the morning and spending time praying and meditating to prepare myself for the day ahead. There were plenty of days that I sat in hospital waiting rooms with a 4-year-old waiting for my dad to get treated. There were days I didn't want to get out of the bed because I didn't know if my dad was going to survive his illness, but I couldn't show my concern to him. There were times where I had to explain to my son why Pop-Pop had to stay in the hospital instead of come home with us. When the times got really rough for me, I would have conversations with God telling Him my problems and asking for guidance and without fail He would show me what to do. Most of the time He would give me a song that would calm my spirit and then thoughts would just come to me or people would talk to me about the very thing I had talked to God about.

I believe the reason prayer is so effective is because it requires you to slow down, surrender and listen for the answer. As women, we can become so consumed with our duties and responsibilities that we are always moving. When you set aside a dedicated time for prayer and meditation you are forcing yourself to be still. It is my desire that every woman take at least 10 minutes a day to spend in prayer and meditation. This may require you to wake up a few minutes earlier or go to bed later. I am confident that the results you receive will make the investment worthwhile. You will be a much calmer mother, wife, friend and worker if you invest in yourself.

How much time are you willing to set aside for prayer and meditation?

....

What time will you pray or meditate each day? Set an appointment with yourself.

....

Keep a journal documenting any prayer requests, thoughts or ideas that are revealed during your prayer time. Start here.

....

....

....

....

....
....
....
....
....
....
....
....

Congratulations!

You have completed the LIFT Yourself 21-day Challenge. You've read and reflected and now it's time to take action. I hope that through slowing down and writing down your dreams, challenges and lessons, you've been inspired to LIFT yourself.

You can live the life you were meant to live. Re-read this book and your answers to the questions whenever you need a quick LIFT.

Let's encourage each other. Together we all can be Living in Freedom and Truth. Contact me at jp@junepinkney.com and let me know how LIFT has helped you.

Acknowledgments

Andre, my son, it's because of you that I have learned so many lessons in the last 21 years of motherhood. Thank you for understanding me and allowing me to impart my wisdom to you. I love you more than you will ever know.

Nikki, my sister, thank you for making me laugh and providing comic relief while I was writing this book.

To my nieces, *Brandi*, *Tyshera* and *Tahnee*, and my nephews *Kyron* and *James* — Thank you for allowing me to assist you at various points in your life. I know I am your Aunt, but you are definitely my children and I am so proud of each of you. Helping you has motivated me to move towards my purpose to help others.

And finally, to my coach, *Jonathan Sprinkles*. Thank you for believing in me even when I didn't believe in myself.

ARE YOU READY TO LIFT YOUR LIFE?

June Pinkney's practical style gives women the skills needed to shift into a higher level of thinking, a higher level of planning and increased performance. A highly sought-after motivational speaker, June provides live and virtual presentations to corporations, associations, women's groups, and youth.

TOPICS:

- Women's empowerment
- Managing family and career
- Personal leadership and development
- Female corporate leadership
- Inspiring performance
- Team- building strategies

*"June Pinkney is an expert in LIFTing yourself and your career from one level to the next. **Listen to her!**"*

Jonathan Sprinkles
"America's Connection Coach"
TV Personality, Two-time Bestselling author

BOOK JUNE TODAY!
215-439-0873

- jp@Junepinkney.com
- Junepinkney-Lift
- www.junepinkney.com

www.ingramcontent.com/pod-product-compliance
Lightning Source LLC
Chambersburg PA
CBHW050656160426
43194CB00010B/1961